Julian Armitstead

After the Accident

Methuen Drama

Published by Methuen Drama 2011

Methuen Drama, an imprint of Bloomsbury Publishing Plc

1 3 5 7 9 10 8 6 4 2

Methuen Drama
Bloomsbury Publishing Plc
36 Soho Square
London W1D 3QY
www.methuendrama.com

First published by Methuen Drama in 2011

ISBN: 978 1 408 15533 2

A CIP catalogue record for this book is available from the British Library

Available in the USA from Bloomsbury Academic & Professional, 175 Fifth
Avenue/3rd Floor, New York, NY 10010. www.BloomsburyAcademicUSA.com

Typeset by Mark Heslington Ltd, Scarborough, North Yorkshire

REM Projects

presents

After the Accident

by Julian Armitstead

After the Accident was first produced by Theatre West
at The Alma Tavern, Bristol in 2009

This production was developed in association with
The North Wall Arts Centre in Oxford, where it
premiered on 1 April 2011 before touring to:
The Brewery Theatre, Tobacco Factory, Bristol
Arc Theatre, Wiltshire
Soho Theatre, London

Funded by Arts Council England

LOTTERY FUNDED

Cast

Frances Ashman
James Kozlowski
Richard Stacey

Creative Team

Writer	**Julian Armitstead**
Director	**Caroline Hunt**
Designer	**Katie Sykes**
Composer	**John O'Hara**
Lighting Designer	**Aaron J. Dootson**
Production Manager	**Luke Peck**
Producer	**REM Projects**
Executive Producer	**Peter James Hall**

Thanks to:
Alison Comley, Ann Stiddard, Dan Danson, North Wall Arts
Centre, Tobacco Factory Theatre, Bristol Old Vic, June
Burrough & The Pierian Centre, Puppet Place, Soho Theatre
and Theatre Bristol

Cast

Frances Ashman

Frances trained at the Guildhall School of Music and Drama. She has worked with the Royal Shakespeare Company in roles including Dorcas in *The Winter's Tale*, Dionyza in *Pericles* and Young Witch in *Macbeth*. Other stage credits include the Mother in *Pornography* (Birmingham Rep, Traverse Theatre, Tricycle Theatre) and Mmoma in *Cockroach* (National Theatre of Scotland, Traverse Theatre). Television credits include Christine in *Dr Who* (BBC Wales – 2010), Susie Bryson in *Gunrush* (ITV – 2007), Teresa Berwick in *Law & Order* (Kudos & ITV – 2009) and Jan Morgan in *Missing* (Leopardrama & BBC – 2008)

James Kozlowski

James started performing with Bristol Old Vic Youth Theatre. Productions included *Fuente Ovejuna* and *The Ice Palace* which played in the Olivier at the National Theatre as part of the Shell Connections festival. At QEH Theatre productions include the *School for Wives*, *The Trial*, *Gormenghast* and *Woyzeck*. Most recently working with Myrtle Theatre Company, performed in *City of One* at the Tobacco Factory which was later performed to an audience of ministers in London.

Richard Stacey

Richard has worked extensively on stage and screen, regularly performing at Oxford Playhouse and with Alan Ayckbourn at the Stephen Joseph Theatre. Credits include: the King in both *Jack and The Beanstalk* & *Sleeping Beauty* (Oxford Playhouse) Andy Rollinson in *Haunting Julia,* Martin in *Life and Beth* (Stephen Joseph Theatre) Bob Phillips in *How The Other Half Loves* (Peter Hall Company/Theatre Royal Bath Productions), Frank Rocco in *Under The Whaleback* (Royal Court). Film & TV Credits include: *Atonement* (Tallis Pictures 2006), Carl Smith in *Evil Elvis* (Rebellion Films 2000), Mr Scott in *The Return of Tracey Beaker* (BBC TV 2009) and Pete Forrister in *Doctors* (BBC TV 2007).

Creative Team

Writer – Julian Armitstead

Julian trained as an actor at the Welsh College of Music and Drama, before becoming a teacher of English and Drama in his late twenties. *After the Accident* was first developed while on attachment at the Birmingham Rep, and subsequently with the help of Arts Council England. It was the winner of the 2008 Amnesty International 'Protect the Human' playwriting competition, and an adapted version was commissioned by BBC Radio 4 for the Friday Play, in a production starring Jack O'Connell and Lia Williams. Julian currently works as a writer in residence in a prison.

Director – Caroline Hunt

Caroline trained LAMDA, NT and RSC as an actor. Films: *Fahrenheit 451* (dir. Francois Truffaut), *Blow Up* (dir. Michelangelo Antonioni). Also Caroline Bone in *The Archers*. Script reader for RSC, Arts Council, Abbey Theatre Dublin. Formed new writing company. Work includes: first production of *A Little Like Drowning* by Anthony Minghella. Productions include: *Lags* by Ron Hutchinson (Tobacco Factory and BAC) and *The Beau* (Bath Theatre Royal and Royal Haymarket). *Head/Case* by Ron Hutchinson (RSC Swan and Soho Theatre) and *Topless Mum* at the Tricycle.

Designer – Katie Sykes

Katie is a highly experienced theatre maker based in Bristol. She has been involved in a number of critically acclaimed productions with companies such as Travelling Light (*How Cold My Toes*, *Shadowplay* and *Boing!*), The Bristol Old Vic (*We're Going on a Bear Hunt* and *Aesop's Fables*), The Tobacco Factory (*The Ugly Duckling* and *Ali Baba & the Forty Thieves*). She has recently set up Shoofly Theatre with Craig Edwards and they are currently touring the company's first family show *Two Four Six Eight!*

Composer – John O'Hara

John is a Composer and Musical Director based in Bristol. He studied at the Royal Northern College of Music and won the Philip Jones prize. He has composed *Merman King*, *Magic Voices* and *The Boy Who Went To The West Wind* for the Welsh National Opera and has a commission from them for 20011/12. He was the resident Composer and Musical Director at the Bristol Old Vic for 11 years. In TV and Radio he has composed for Channel 4, Channel 5, HTV, Radio 4 and the BBC and has performed on numerous sessions for BBC and independent TV. He plays Piano and Accordion in the Rock Band *Jethro Tull*.

Lighting Designer – Aaron J. Dootson

Aaron graduated from Wimbledon College of Art in 2009 where he studied Lighting Design and Practice qualifying with a distinction. Aaron is a freelance lighting designer specialising in theatre, based mainly in London. Theatre credits include *74 Georgia Avenue* (New End Theatre), *Tipping Point* (Bristol Hamilton House/ New Wimbledon Studio), *Bluebird* (Cockpit Theatre), *This Is How It Goes* (Kings Head Theatre), *Siren* (Etcetera Theatre), *Leo You Nutter* (Wimbledon College of Art) and *Tape* (North Outlet Theatre Company). He has also worked with Impact Dance on a series of shows including *Extract*, *Smash* and *Strangers*. www.aaronjdootson.co.uk

Production Manager – Luke Peck

Luke is a Production Manager and Lighting Technician based in Bristol. He has worked extensively in the South West and beyond on a range of productions including: *Swallows and Amazons*, *Juliet and Her Romeo* & *Far Away* (Bristol Old Vic), *Sleeping Beauty* (Theatre Royal Bath), *Anthony and Cleopatra* & *Julius Caesar* (Shakespeare at The Tobacco Factory) He has also supported numerous smaller companies including Full Beam Visual Theatre, Pangottic and Theatre West.

Producer – REM Projects

REM Projects is Rachel McNally and Nastasia Tryphonos. They specialise in working with touring theatre companies creating innovative work for all ages. Productions include: *After the Accident* by Julian Armitstead, Full Beam Visual Theatre *(My Baby Just Cares For Me, The Lesser Spotted Collectors' Club, The Man Who Discovered That Women Lay Eggs)*, Pickled Image *(Houdini's Suitcase, Wolf Tales, Travels with Granddad)*, The Devil's Violin Company *(The Singing*

Bones), Shoofly Theatre *(Two, Four, Six, Eight!)* and Myrtle Theatre Company *(Up Down Boy)*. They are also part of the production team for Bristol Festival of Puppetry.
www.remprojects.com

Executive Producer – Peter James Hall
Peter has been involved with numerous music and film productions. He is a member of the Sydney Film Festival Council, the Sydney Theatre Company and the Director's Circle of the Old Vic. He is also founder and Chairman of the leading ethical investment company Hunter Hall and an anti-whaling and biodiversity activist.

What The Writer and Director Say:

Julian Armitstead (writer)

"I learned about Restorative Justice several years before I decided to write a play about it. Around that time I was teaching in a prison, and sensed in the basic premise of the idea an insight of such obvious humanity and sense, that I thought that some writer somewhere should be bringing it to the attention of a wider audience. And the premise is this: that sometimes, and within the right structures, it can be of enormous benefit to the victim of a crime to meet with the offender.

But how easy could it be to do this? Or rather, how difficult? And to whose benefit, really? That's what I set out to explore."

Caroline Hunt (director)

"After the Accident is a fantastic play to work on. It's the story of a car crash and the death of a child, told from the point of view of three characters. The boy in prison who caused the crash and the parents of the child, and how the story changes when they meet through Restorative Justice and the responsibility for the accident shifts from one to another. The actors have a big journey to make through the play. It's a great story and Julian uses a device that allows the audience to get right into the argument and keeps them guessing. You only have to look at the way the text is laid down on the page to realise the rhythms of the language and the energy of the words. There are very clear movements and changes of pace. It's the nearest I'll get to working on a piece of orchestral music. Julian has an absolute commitment to big emotion and the actors have to go for it, they have to be brave. Each of the characters has their own very clear voice and speech patterns so the characters are found in the language too. Because it's quite intense we have to look for the contrasts, the resting places and the laughs. It's great for us to have so many layers to work on."

After the Accident

Characters

Leon, *a boy of nineteen*
Petra, *a woman in her early/mid forties, a journalist*
Jimmy, *a man in his early/mid forties, a teacher*

And the voices of:
Mr E, *the prison art teacher*
Leon's mum
(*These characters are portrayed by the actors playing* **Jimmy** *and* **Petra** *respectively.*)

After the Accident is set around the outworking of a restorative justice process, from before to after a conference. It is set in the present day.

Author's note

The play makes use of the convention of simultaneous dialogue. To indicate this, speech *ending* with (/) continues into the next piece of speech by the same character.

The layout of the text reflects the way in which the voices first emerged, neither randomly, nor consistently, but in a constant struggle for the centre. Having revised it to a more conventional prose format for the purposes of radio, I was asked by the actors and cast of the subsequent stage production to return it again to the original. From which I can only suppose, that this is how the characters intended it. Make of it what you will.

Scene One

The stage is bare except for three chairs standing in approximate symmetry across the stage.

Leon

So this is what happened:
Freddie comes to my window,
Starts chucking stones against the glass.
Must have been about
Eight o'clock
Friday night.
'We're going fishing,'
Says Freddie.
And he holds out this piece of kit:
This fishing rod in three pieces.
And at first
I think he's having a laugh
Cos we're a long way from the sea.

Jimmy
(as from an ante room, before the conference)
Before we enter the room
Casey talks to us outside,
All lowered voices:
'The thing about a
Restorative conference,'
He says,
'We're all here to learn.
We're all here to listen.'
Well:
I'm listening.
I'm listening.

Leon

There was this place called the strip.
It was just a piece of land behind a warehouse.
They was going to build on it, once they got permission.

They was going to develop the whole place.
Tesco's,
Brantano's,
JJB.
Freddie said
All we needed was
A burger drive-in –

(*Stops himself; beat.*)

But that's not funny any more.

Petra
(*surveying the conference*)
So it's just chairs facing each other.
Casey sits in the middle.
The boy opposite
And next to the boy,
His supporter.
He's only got the one:
Since no one from his family's
Managed to turn up,
He's got this social worker instead.

Leon
So I remember how it was:
Freddie and me.
Sometimes when we was bunking school,
But best of all
Was late at night.
Cos this place,
It had tarmac,
And concrete,
And fields at the end.
And that's when we first saw what you can do:
Handbrake turns at forty mile an hour,
Young blokes bringing cars,
Spinning them around like tops,
It's like the wacky races I'm telling you.

> Except when they've finished using them,
> They torch them,
> Cover their traces.
> And once you've seen that – /

Petra
And I want to tell her:
'I don't want blood –

> **Leon**
> Once you've smelled that/

Petra
An eye for an eye
Making the whole world blind' /

> **Leon**
> What half a gallon of petrol in the back seat can do
> When you chuck in a match.

Petra
'But when it comes to a life;
The life of your own child – '

> **Leon**
> Well:
> What else comes near?

Petra
(*to the conference*)
Stop.
Please.
Mr Casey?
I think I need a time out.

> **Jimmy**
> Time out!
> Anyone can call a time out

At any moment in the conference.
It's like –
Waving your little red card at the teacher.

Petra
I'm sorry, Jimmy.
It's doing my head in.
Seeing *him* here and everything.
I'll be all right in a moment.

Scene Two

Jimmy *and* **Petra** *move out of the setting of the conference. As they place themselves on stage, we are aware that these are private, parallel monologues, mediated perhaps through the context of individual therapy.*

Jimmy
Time out.

(*Beat.*)

OK.
Here's a memory.
Three years after,
After the accident.
I'm waking up early.
Well,
There's this sodding pigeon
Cooing from the bottom of the garden.

(*Beat.*)

So I have this idea:
I'm going to get my dad's shotgun down from the loft,
I'm going to take it down
And shoot the fucker,
Cos it's driving me nuts.

(*Beat.*)

But when I get outside,
The sun's streaming through the trees,
And there's been a late frost:
This patina of frost all over the back garden.

Petra
Memory.
Here's another:
One year before,
Before –

(*Beat; she won't name it.*)

Well,
We move house.

(*To* **Charley**, *a mother again.*)

You remember, Charley?
She's five,
And you do:
You remember things at that age.
You lay down memories like a new wine.
And I want her to remember everything,
So she can write about it when she goes to school:
'The Day We Moved House',
By Charley.

Leon
So this is how it happened:

Petra
No./

Leon
We walk for half a mile.

Petra
No!
I haven't finished!/

Leon
We walk for about half a mile,
Freddie and me,
Till we come to this place.

Petra
I won't.
I can't.
I'm not listening!

Jimmy
So I'm thinking:
'I'm not going into work
On a morning like this.'
And I just get into the car
And start driving.

Leon
It's a luxury development,
We pass it every morning
On the way to school.
It's got a name on a sign outside.
It's got a gate.
And around the gate
It's got this wall.
The only thing it hasn't got
Is a lake and a fiery dragon.
And the things you can see through there:
Four-by-fours,
Turbo convertibles –
It's like Top Gear,
I'm telling you:
The specs on those cars.
You want to put your hands all over them.
And that's why they got the walls, right?
Cos they're expecting you to try.

Petra
(*lost in her thoughts*)
So I'm pointing things out to her
All the while:
Look, Charley.
The van's pulling up!
Look, Charley.
Dad's about to open the front door.
Smell that, Charley!

Jimmy
Past woodland.
Hills.
One time I have to stop the car.
There's this field of bluebells.
I want to get out and walk.
Take my shoes and socks off.
Get my toes wet.
God!
The world can be so beautiful.

(*Beat.*)

But instead I'm on the motorway again.
Getting off at junction nine.

Petra
What's that sound, Charley?
We're all sat at the bottom of the stairs listening.
It's like holding a shell so close to your ear that you can hear the sea.
Even the removal men can hear it.
What's that?
Can you hear that, Charley?
That's the sound of an empty house!
But what's it saying?
What's it saying?

Leon
We're hanging there for about an hour
When this Mini Cooper comes in the drive.
Young bloke,
Yuppie in a suit.
And out of the passenger seat
Comes this girl.

(*Beat.*)

Well, Freddie gives me the elbow,
You know,
As they go in.
And we're waiting
Five,
Ten minutes
When the light goes on in the bedroom.

(*Beat.*)

The girl looks out.
She's standing there in the window.
She's let her hair down.
She's in this gown,
This red gown.
And we're both wanting her to take it off
Like you do, you know,
When the bloke comes up behind her
And takes her back behind the curtains.

Jimmy
I find my way along an A road
To this village.
Looks nice enough.
Pub on the right-hand side,
Signpost.
Almost miss it,
In fact I do,
I do miss it.
Have to turn back on myself.

Then it's down a lane
Bare trees either side,
Till the lane turns into this:
Driveway.

(*Beat.*)

And there it is.
Christ.
And though it's larger than I'd imagined,
In other ways
It's just how you do imagine it.
A place like that,
With razor wire over the top.

(*Beat.*)

I park up.
Five minutes.
Ten.
Half an hour.
You hear what I'm saying?
Till I find myself sitting there for three,
Four hours,
Just looking at the sodding gate.
Thinking all the time:
'He'll be coming through there.
He'll be coming through that gate there.'

(*Small pause.*)

Then someone knocks at my window.

Petra
'Hello,
Can I help you?' says the house.
'I hope so,'
We say.
'We've come to live here:
Me, Charley, Jimmy,
We've come here to stay!
We've come here to be happy!'

Leon
And from that moment:
Well, I'm still seeing her.
So's Freddie, I reckon,
Though he don't say nothing.
That bloke pulling the girl back
Makes me feel so
Horny,
Not just for her,
But for every inch of what he had.
Made me feel
So
Like:
I've got to have something of his now.
I've got to take something of his now.

Petra
Stop.

Jimmy
(*relentless*)
Here's another memory:

Petra
No,
Stop, please!

Jimmy
Can't stop!
Another memory!

(*Beat.*)

We went to the sea that summer.
The summer after we moved house.
She had a ride on this donkey.
Next thing we know
She's wanting a pony of her own!

(*Beat.*)

So I take her to a stable
And let her stroke the foal.
Petra takes a picture.

(*Beat.*)

Then Charley says:

Petra
(*not as* **Charley**, *but rather as herself, fondly remembering*)
'I want it,
I want it, Daddy!'

Jimmy
So I say:
'But you know what, Charley?
I want, I want
Can't always have!'

Petra
'But I want it, Daddy!'

Jimmy
No, Charley!

Petra
'Then I'm not going home!
I'm not going home!
I'm not going home
Without Horsey!'

Jimmy
Horsey?
Horsey?

(*Suddenly fearsome.*)

I'll give you bloody Horsey!

Petra
Jimmy, no!
No.
Stop.
Stop.

Jimmy
(*small pause; softer now*)
So I say to her:
I say to her:
'Maybe when you're older, Charley.
Maybe when you're ten,
Eleven.
You know?
You know?'

Scene Three

Leon *in jail. Tentative, at arm's length, as if introducing a tableau of his own making.*

Leon
When I go down.

(*Beat.*)

When I go down,
My mum shoots me this look:
'I can't help you now, son.
Don't blame this on me.
You're on your own now, boy.'
She says it all,
With the eyes.
Just with the eyes.

(*Then, turning to* **Petra**.)

Then the woman stands up:

Petra
(*turning to him*)
Murderer!
He's a bloody murderer!

Jimmy
(*drawing her back*)
Petra.

Leon
And I want to say something back,
I have to say something!

Petra
(*as if to the whole world*)
But he needs to know.
Someone needs to tell him
If the court bloody won't!

Leon
Then screw you!
Fuck you!

The moment is briefly held: **Leon** *his fingers in the air,* **Petra** *and*
Jimmy *watching.*

Scene Four

Jimmy *moves into next scene, his first, preliminary meeting, alone*
with **Casey***, the victim liaison officer cum RJ facilitator.*

Jimmy
And that was the last we saw of him,
Mr Casey
Four years ago in court.
I remember it like it was yesterday.
And to be honest,

If I allow myself to experience now
What I was feeling then:
Christ!
I want to kill him.
I just want to kill him.

(*Beat.*)

But you know:
It's all very well,
This idea of us
All sitting in a room together,
Even supposing we could get that far.
Even supposing I could get Petra
To see the need.

(*Beat.*)

Well, even then,
The things
We could say:
They'd just be the things we could say.
You know?
Cos what we really want,
I don't think
We know how to take.

(*Beat.*)

It's not an apology we're after.
And it's not
Painting our garden fence for a couple hours on a Saturday
morning.
We'd be there
Because we needed to see his face,
Before we have to catch a glimpse of him
Walking down the street with a girl on his arm,
Or coming out of a pub
Singing.
Do you think he sings, Mr Casey?
Do you?

Do you think he sings in the shower?
Or when the sun shines outside?
Because we don't.
We don't sing any more.

(*Beat.*)

Not since
There's nothing to sing about.

Scene Five

Leon *in jail, somewhere near the beginning of his custodial sentence.*

Leon
Eight do four.
Eight do four.

(*Beat.*)

Lawyer says:
'Could have been worse, Leon,
Could have been fourteen.'
Fourteen?
Course that's fourteen do seven.
Everything cut in half like.
Like my mate.
Like Freddie.

(*Beat.*)

Mr E says:
'You have something of value,
Leon.
You just got to go find it, that's all.
And there are things here that can help you do that:
Opportunities right here.'
I say,
'Bollocks.

Just biding my time, mate:
Eight do four,
Eight do four!'
Do you get me?

(*Beat.*)

Hard case, me.
PYO:
Persistent Young Offender.
One count of burglary,
One count of taking without owner's consent.
One count of driving without a licence,
Two counts of causing death by dangerous driving.
Sixty-five previous offences to be taken into consideration.

(*Beat.*)

Have you ever seen someone cut in half?
Pair of legs!
So don't look at me like that.
I said,
Don't look at me like that!

(*Small pause.*)

We didn't go looking for her, all right?
We're not:
What they say.
We're not:
That thing.

(*Beat; then with sudden vulnerability.*)

It was an accident.
But you won't read that in the papers, will you.
Fucking hell.
There's a lot you won't read in the papers.

Scene Six

Jimmy *and* **Petra** *at the therapist, a couples session.*

Jimmy
(explanatory, to the audience)
Couples session.
Three months before the conference.

Pause, waiting for something to come up. Then **Petra** *starts up, as if out of nowhere:*

Petra
I had a funny conversation the other day.
Veronica,
This childhood friend.
Well, she came over for the day.
I hadn't seen her in years.
In our youth
We were always fighting.
You know the kind of thing:
When you have a mate,
Who's like,
The nearest thing you have to a sister.

(Beat.)

Well, anyway,
We both fancied this boy.
This gorgeous young monkey.
Don't know what it was about him.
Must have been his arse,
Cos I don't remember his conversation.
But she's the one to get the date.
She always is,
While I'm hiding out in some corner.

(Beat.)

So one afternoon,
While she's putting on this lip gloss that I've bought her

For the very purpose of entertaining His Gorgeousness:
While her back is turned,
I smear something on her hairbrush.
Something so foul
I can scarcely believe
I'm doing it!
Oh, God,
How old was I at the time,
Jimmy?

Jimmy
You were fifteen.

Petra
Well, that's thirty years ago!
And I remember it like yesterday.
Funny thing is,
When she came back from her date,
She never says a word.
Not one word!

(*Beat.*)

Well, this little act of sabotage
Maybe I'm imagining it,
But it seemed to coincide
With an extraordinary reversal
In our respective fortunes.
Because from that day on,
And I kid you not,
While I become the achiever,
The successful journalist and wife
You see before you,
Veronica hangs back in the shadows,
As though life
Refuses to release her from her starting box.

Jimmy
That's a bit unfair.

Petra
Well she's had a bloody time of it.

Jimmy
We've all had a bloody time of it.

Petra
All right!

Jimmy
So why bring it up?

Petra
Anyway,
I heard nothing more about that boy,
Until,
A couple of weeks ago:
Veronica and I
We meet up.
And at the end of a particularly intense discussion
About the different paths life has taken us,
And about what's happened since –

(*Beat – she won't say it.*)

You know.
About all this
Therapy
We're taking,
This endless round of conversation.
I tell her how Jimmy wants us
To meet
The young toe-rag who did this to us.
How Jimmy's got this
Bee in his bonnet,
This bit
Between his teeth.
And I can feel the compassion welling up in her:
This unbearable

Sense of pity.
And I want to say:
'For God's sake, Veronica,
For God's sake!'

Jimmy
Is this supposed to make you feel better?

Petra
Isn't that what we're here for?
To talk.
About anything
And everything?
To communicate:
To get things moving?

(*Beat.*)

So instead I say:
'You remember that boy?'
And I mention his name.
I can even remember his name!
Steven!
It was Steven!

Jimmy
No.
That's not his name.
That's not his name!

Petra
And I even tell her what I did.
I tell her:
'If he didn't like you, Veronica,
It must have been because of what
You smelled of:'

Jimmy
He's called Leon./

Petra
'Dog shit!'/

Jimmy
The boy she can't stop thinking of.
He's called Leon./

Petra
(*savage, now*)
'Dog shit!'

(*beat*)

Well, after the shock of it
We were both able to laugh./

Jimmy
And now
To make matters worse
She's annoyed
I've got this bloke
From Victim Liaison
Coming round tomorrow.

Petra
I think we both felt comforted by the experience.
Elated,
That we still had this shared memory.
That there were still things to explore.

(*Beat.*)

So that's all I wanted to say.
Friendships are so important.
Trust.
Don't you think, Jimmy?

Jimmy
I think the counsellor's
Astute enough to realise

What's important.
Like I said:

Petra
You see
Jimmy's arranged for this man:
This man
To come round with some art work.
Art work!/

Jimmy
He's bringing us a letter
And a couple of pictures./

Petra
As if
That's somehow supposed to help us understand
The boy who did this./

Jimmy
Me,
I'd run naked through the streets
If it offered us a way forward.

Petra
But I don't want to understand,
Because
Understanding is always a prelude to forgiving.
Isn't it?
So he gets out scot free
While we're stuck in here?
He could turn up
On our doorstep.

Jimmy
But he's coming out
Whether we like it or not.

Petra
I could bump into him
At Sainsbury's.
You know,
I'm actually thinking of moving
To Australia!

Jimmy
We're not moving anywhere!
We're not going anywhere!
We just need to talk.

Petra
But we've been talking solidly.

Jimmy
About the person,
Petra,
The person
Who did *this* to us.
No!
You've been talking solidly –

Petra
Well maybe
You should speak up more.

Jimmy
About nothing!
I'm not even allowed to mention his name.

(*To the shrink.*)

You must have noticed,
She won't allow me to mention his name.

Petra
Well,
Apparently the process is called/

Jimmy
It's not important what they call it./

> **Petra**
> Restorative Justice.
> And that's a laugh.

Jimmy
I said,
It's not important what they call it!

> **Petra**
> Oh, I think
> Names are important,
> Otherwise how are we supposed to know
> What's in the tin?
> So what I want to ask is:/

Jimmy
Well I want to give it a go,
All right?

> **Petra**
> Where's the justice?/

Jimmy
I just want *us* to give it a go.

> **Petra**
> And what exactly does it restore to us?
> I mean for God's sake:
> What can we conceivably have back from him
> That we could possibly accept?

Jimmy
I don't know!
I don't know,
All right?

But what else is there?
No, you tell me:
What else is there?

Pause, as **Jimmy** *leaves.* **Petra** *is alone now with the counsellor.*

Petra
There!
He always does that.
Do you see?
When the temperature rises,
When it gets too much,
He just ups and goes.

(*Beat.*)

Well you can see what that's supposed to achieve,
Can't you?
How he's trying to paint me into a corner?

(*Beat.*)

Anyway,
They call it
Shuttle mediation.
This first stage.
Like a kind of judicial foreplay,
Before we really
Get to grips.
You know:

(*Beat.*)

There's this
Facilitator
Who talks to us,
Then goes back to the boy.
Talks to the boy,
Then comes back to us.
Back and forth,
Weaving and bobbing

Like the busy little shuttle he is,
To see if there's any common desire
For a meeting.

(*Beat.*)

Well, there isn't.
Why should there be?
I don't want to be woven.
I'm not a bloody carpet.
I'm not here to help.

(*Beat.*)

God knows,
I'm here,
Because I'm here.

(*Small pause.*)

Oh, sod it!

Scene Seven

Jimmy *and* **Petra***'s living room.*

Jimmy
(*mock-grandiose, to the audience*)
The day the man came round.

And suddenly, **Petra** *and* **Jimmy** *are preparing to welcome the invisible* **Casey**, *for what is to be their first preparatory meeting with him as a couple.*

Petra*'s mood is profoundly resistant: petulant; light-headed with alcohol and depression. Yet at the same time, an absurd humour lies just underneath their perception of this controlled domestic arrangement.*

Jimmy
(*wry, almost enjoying himself*)
He's on time,
This bloke.
He's so on time
I think he's been standing outside our front door
With a stop-watch.
Do you know what I mean?

Petra
The day the man came round
I find myself tidying the place up.
Uncharacteristically, fluffing up cushions,
Hoovering behind the sofa.
And since it's just turned April,
I put some daffs in a vase.

(*Beat.*)

And then I think:
That's it.
That'll do for a spring-clean.

Jimmy
Then at six o'clock precisely –

Petra
When the doorbell rings, Jimmy lets him in.
Six in the evening.
But it's still light,
Now that the clocks have moved forward.
I stand up but I'm not moving.
Cos I'm thinking:
I'll tidy the place up,
But I'm not giving the wrong impression.

Jimmy
He's a wiry little fella,
Short grey hair and a tash.

Neat, square face:
Earring –
You know?

(*Beat.*)

He's holding a yellow cyclist's jacket under his arm,
And this
Blue plastic helmet.

Petra
And he doesn't wait to be asked.
Sees me standing in the corner,
Like some sulking child at her own party.
'I'm Casey,' he says.
'Call me Casey,
As in, Casey the case-worker.'
And he holds out his hand.

Jimmy
So Petra chirps up,
'Shouldn't that be Frankie?
As in Frankie the friendly facilitator?'
With an edge, you know.
Cos she's already had a drink.
So I put my arm round her,
Protective,
But at the same time,
You know:
'Don't embarrass me, Petra,
The bloke's a guest.
We both of us invited him here.
You agreed.'

Petra
Then Jimmy sort of pushes me down into the settee.
I'm feeling heady,
Ever so slightly pissed,
Like I've drunk half a bottle of that

Sweet white I bought on my way back from the office.
Though matter of fact,
It's the memory of that cherry blossom down the bottom of
our road.
Cos when you see that,
There are lights all the way down your spine, saying:
'Winter should be over.
Winter should be over.'

(*Beat; then flinching.*)

Christ!

Jimmy
Then he opens this bag.

Petra
Oh Christ!

Jimmy
Takes out this folder.

Petra
(*faltering, refusing*)
Look:
I don't know.
I don't know if I can –

Jimmy
'That's him,' he says.
'That's Leon.
Bit of a Rembrandt really,
Since he discovered his art.'

(*Beat. Then to her, as* **Jimmy** *again, concerned.*)

Petra – ?

Petra
(*to* **Casey**, *frigid with anger*)
Who gave you permission to use his name in here?

Scene Eight

Leon in his jail art class, early in the fourth year of his sentence. He's displaying his work, which we imagine, perhaps hung on the back wall. His enthusiasm is all too apparent: childish in its freshness, but tinged with acute self-consciousness of what others might say or think.

Leon
(grandly, announcing)
'Around the World in Eighty Days!'

(Beat.)

That was Mr E's idea.
A series of pictures of Yours Truly
In different places –
Places he's never been.
For example,
Here I am driving this car across Africa,
Trying not to hit the giraffes.

(Sensing a titter.)

Don't laugh.
Don't bloody laugh!

(Beat. Picking up confidence.)

It's all,
Holes in the ground,
And you've got to take your own food and water.
Watch out for sandstorms and flash floods.
Scorpions there, look!
You see the logo on that vehicle?
Well, that was Mr E's idea and all:
Save the Children.
Save the Children!

(Beat.)

I've seen it all on TV:

Sponsorship deal worth millions.
Picture in the paper.
Interviewed by Jeremy Clarkson!

(*Beat.*)

But you don't cross Africa by yourself,
It's too dangerous.
So you got to take a mate with you.
And that's him there, look:
In the passenger seat.

(*Beat.*)

Me,
I wasn't too sure,
But Mr E said:

Mr E
Sure,
If that's how you feel, Leon,
Why not!

Leon
So I've sewn him back together.
He's got a belt on this time.

Scene Nine

Back at **Jimmy** *and* **Petra**'s. *They have just seen the picture.*

Petra
(*explosive*)
Well bollocks to that!
I mean,
What he's done;
What he's done to us:

Jimmy
So he draws cars, does he?

Petra
It doesn't go away, you know,
It doesn't diminish.

Jimmy
Art therapy?
Now that's one we haven't tried.

Petra
He can draw cars all he likes.

Jimmy
Petra, the gentleman's only here to help.
He's trying to give us a sense of the lad.

Petra
When I got the message:
I want you to imagine this.
No, I want you to *see* this:

Jimmy
Love,
No one's forcing us to do this.

Petra
When the police come round with the news,
I've been sat here for over an hour and a half,
Mr Casey.

Jimmy
(*to* **Casey**)
Look, mate,
I'm sorry.

Petra
Sorry?
Sorry?

Jimmy
OK, Petra,
Calm down, will you!

                              Petra
                    So he draws cars instead of crashing them?
                              Well that's nice.

                              (*To* **Casey**.)

                    But, with the greatest respect,
                    It was Jimmy who invited you here.
                              Not me!

Jimmy
So she gets up,
And we all know what's going on now:
She's trying to make a pig of herself,
She wants to wallow!
She wants to roll around in it!

                              Petra
                        I go to the kitchen,
                    While Jimmy and the man Casey
                              Sit there./

Jimmy
So I say to the bloke:/

                              Petra
                        I'm shaking with it
                              The rage,
                        The bitterness of it,
                        The bloody unfairness./

Jimmy
'Now perhaps you can see –
And it's probably just as well –
The reason I invited you here

To talk to you about the lad.
It's not that we forgive him,
Because we can't,
We can't do that.
But I'm fed up with him
Having this power,
This power over us.'

Petra
And I know it's Easter,
It *is* that time of year.
But fuck it.
Put me in a room with him,
Put me in a room with that bastard and a set of nails
And I'd show him what it's like to be hung out to dry.
I'd pick up my hammer and nails,
Two large ones for his hands
And a stake for his feet
And Bang!
Bang! Bang! Bang! Bang! Bang!
I'd nail him to his fucking easel!

Jimmy
So I have to hand it to him.
That Casey.
Cos when Petra goes into the kitchen
And I start apologising
He doesn't bat an eye.
He just gets up
And walks towards the kitchen.
'Can you make that two?'
He says.
'Do you mind if I join you in a glass?'
So I say
'Mine's a lemonade, mate,
Cos I don't drink.
But make that three glasses
And we'll all have something to hold in our hands.'

(*Beat.*)

And then,
Maybe I'm mistaken,
But I feel something changing
In the air.
You know;
Something like spring,
Like:
Electricity discharging,
Like:
The first thunder's
Broken out of the sky.

Petra
(*now suddenly becalmed*)
There.
There!
Calm again.
Anger over.

Jimmy
So I get out the biscuits
And blow me down
If Petra doesn't comes back in with the bottle,
And three glasses!

Petra
(*calmer now, but not without irony*)
Anger over!

(*Beat.*)

I'm sorry.
Forgetting my manners.
What can I say?

(*Beat.*)

But you see, Mr Casey,
Ever since:

Ever since it happened,
I've had this –
Anger.
This –
Monstrous anger.
I don't know how else to put it.

Jimmy
Let me try,
Let me try and explain.

(*Beat.*)

It's been four years
And you might think,
Well –
Four years;
That's a certain amount of water under the bridge.
But when something like this happens
Time –

(*Pause. He is on the very edge of control.*)

Well,
Time stands still.
Cos there's absolutely nothing –
Nothing
Prepares you for it.
It blows you away.
You're nothing,
Zero,
Nada.
And you can multiply anything by zero,
Do you get me?
Anything you like:
Four,
Eight years,
A lifetime.
At the end of it,
What are you left with?

I mean:
What are you left with?

Scene Ten

Leon *in jail, about a year into his term.*

Leon
So one day
My mum comes to visit:
'Freddie's brothers are after you,'
She says.
'They're putting shit into our letter-box.'

(*Beat.*)

'Tight bastards,'
I say.
'Couldn't they afford a stamp?'

(*Beat.*)

'How can you make a joke out of that?'
She says.
'Out of what?' I say.
'Out of what you've done.'

(*Beat.*)

'It's all right, Mum,
I won't come knocking on your door.'
'Bloody right.
Cos you've already pissed all over it.'

(*Beat.*)

And then she starts screaming.

Mum
(*ferocious*)
And you know what they're calling you?
You know what they're bloody calling you?

Leon
(*embarrassed, looking around him*)
All right, Mum.
Stop shouting, will ya?
Everybody's looking!

Mum
Let them look.
Let them fucking look,
I'll tell them and all.

Leon
Go on then!
Go on!

Mum
They're calling you a child-killer.
They're calling you a paedo.

Leon
(*ballistic now*)
You bitch!
You fucking bitch.
That's bollocks./

Mum
Is it?
Is it? /

Leon
That's bollocks
And you know that!
You fucking know it!

Mum
Do I?
Do I?

(*Beat.*)

Well maybe you're right.
Cos what you are is rubbish.
Just rubbish, you.
So don't expect to come home.
Don't expect to come home to me!

Scene Eleven

Leon *in his art class.*

Mr E
So draw rubbish, Leon.
Draw rubbish!

Leon
Like how am I supposed to do that?

Mr E
Anyone can draw rubbish.

Leon
Not me.
I can't.
I can't do bollocks.

Mr E
Who said anything about bollocks?
I'm just asking for rubbish.

Leon
Go away!
Just go away.

Mr E
You got anything better to do?

(*Beat.*)

Do what you like.

Leon
What I like?
Do what I like?
I'll tell you what I like:
I'd like to push this pencil right into my fucking ear hole.

Mr E
Now why do you want to do that?

Leon
Cos it's doing what I like!

Mr E
I can think of better uses for it, Leon.

Leon
Well, maybe that's cos
You're you,
And I'm me.
But if you know it all,
Why don't you tell me?
Do you have to be unlucky to be me?
Or do you just have to be rubbish?

(*He puts the pencil into his ear.*)

Unlucky or rubbish?

Mr E
Don't be daft, Leon./

Leon
Pencil's hurting, Mr E./

Mr E
Don't be so stupid!

Leon
Unlucky or rubbish?

Mr E
Are you going to stop this now, Leon?
Or am I going to have to have to press that alarm button?

(*Beat.*)

Leon!

Leon *takes it out.*

Mr E
Don't you *ever* do that to me again,
You hear?

Leon
(*beat. Subdued now*)
Robbing cars.
That's all I was doing.
That doesn't make me a nonce, does it?
Doesn't make me a kiddy fiddler,
Or a child killer,
Well does it?
Well, fucking does it?

(*Beat.*)

So why me?
Why me!

Mr E
Why not you?
What's all this 'me'?

Leon
What are you talking about?

Mr E
Who's 'me', Leon?
Draw 'me'!

Leon
You should fucking listen to yourself!

> **Mr E**
> (*beat; lighter now*)
> All right:
> You ask,
> '*Why me?*'
> But I say,
> Why *not* you?
> Why not *you*, Leon?
> I mean,
> Welcome to the human bloody race!
>
> (*Beat.*)
>
> Or are you telling me,
> You've never stepped in a steaming pile of dog crap
> And asked exactly the same question?

Scene Twelve

Jimmy *and* **Petra**'s *living room.*

> **Petra**
> (*softly now, with great weariness*)
> When the police bring me the news,
> I'm here.
> This place.
> I've been working late that evening
> At the newspaper,
> My job.
> So when I return home
> About nine, Mr Casey,
> I'm expecting Jimmy to be here,
> Expecting our baby./

Jimmy
She wasn't a baby – /

Petra
To be in bed.
Because since Jimmy and I last spoke – /

Jimmy
(*to* **Casey**)
She was six
Going on thirteen.

Petra
No one has rung me –
No one has rung me to say
What's going on.

Jimmy
You see,
Personally,
During this time,
The hours immediately afterwards,
After the accident:
I wasn't really aware.
I had no real awareness.

Petra
So I did what I always do when I come home late,
At the end of a long week:

(*Begins to enact the homecoming.*)

'Jimmy?'
'Charley?'

Jimmy
For Petra too,
I think this is a time when we only partly exist.

Petra
And when no one answers,
I think:
Well that's strange.

Jimmy

Cos when we want to go back to it,
When we try to go back,
It moves away from us.

Petra

So I check my mobile for messages:

Jimmy

And all I can come up with – /

Petra

Nothing!
Not a dicky bird!

Jimmy

Is the time before the time.
Like the time itself,
The moment itself
Is just a pair of her empty shoes.
And I know that she was walking around in them,
Hours before,
But I can't see her feet.
So I'm asking,
'Where are her feet in those shoes?'

Petra

Must have stopped at Laetitia's, then!
Mind you:

Jimmy

And all I'm left with
Are some last words:

Petra

I can see Charley digging her little heels in.
Doing her party trick.

Jimmy
Some stupid last words
Before we left the party.

(*In recall.*)

'We're off now, Charley.'/

Petra
In the evenings she got so easily overwrought.
The slightest thing could upset her.

Jimmy
'No.
Don't be like that, Charley!'

Petra
And it was no good talking to her
If she just needed to get home!

Jimmy
If you don't come home
Daddy's going to be cross.

(*Beat; amused despite himself.*)

What was that you said?

Petra
Even at that age,
She had a gob on her.

Jimmy
What did you say?
If I had a bar of soap!

Petra
And child-minders were bloody useless.

Jimmy
Who taught you to speak like that like?

Petra
So there was no continuity.
The moment we found one that was any good,
They'd either go away or get ill.

> **Jimmy**
> Five more minutes, babe:
> And then we're off.
> We are
> One hundred per cent going.

(*He freezes, caught in the recollection.*)

Petra
So instead of checking up,
Mr Casey,
Instead of ringing around
Like I should,
I decide,
Sod it!
I'll let Jimmy deal.
I'll let Jimmy cope with this.

> **Jimmy**
> (*emphatically not coping*)
> 'No, you're not sitting in the front seat,
> No way!
> This is your seat, here, Charley.
> In here, I said.
> No, you can't sit next to Daddy,
> Cos Daddy's not allowed.
> Back here's where you sit,
> In your special seat!
> In Charley's magic seat
> With Charley's magic belt:
> The belt with the magical powers!'

Petra
(*recitative almost, recalling* **Charley**)
'But I'm not going home,
I'm not going home,
I'm not going home
Without Horsey!'

Jimmy
'What do you mean,
"You're not going home"?'

Petra
I know it's ridiculous,
Mr Casey.

Jimmy
'You bloody *are* going home:'

Petra
But *Horsey* had become the front seat.

Jimmy
'You're going home with me!'

Petra
So when she wanted to assert herself,
She wanted to be riding Horsey.

(*Small pause.*)

Well, the next thing I know,
It's half past nine, Mr Casey,
And the doorbell's ringing.
I must have dozed off:
I'm still feeling dizzy,
So I let it ring.
It must be Charley,
Playing games,
Or Jimmy being a lazy beggar,
Cos I know he's got the house keys.
But it's not.

Jimmy
'Look,
I only promised you five minutes, babe.'

Petra
Oh, Christ, it's not.

Jimmy
'Then get in that front seat.
Get in that front seat.
And make sure you put your belt on.'

Petra
There are these two police officers
Standing outside our front door
Like ghosts.

Jimmy
(*to* **Petra** *now, feeling her blame*)
Well what else did you expect me to do?
Friday night:
What else did you expect?

Small pause.

Petra
I'm completely numb.
I can hear,
But I can't take it in.
There's this person –
This young WPC –
Telling me.
Telling me.

Scene Thirteen

Leon *in jail. Recent time before the conference.*

Leon
So one day
I get this visit.
This bloke from
Victim Liaison.
Mr Casey.
Casey the case!
He says he's got this proposal.
This bit of news.
And I'm expecting him to say
Something about my parole,
You know:
Something about my chances there.
So I'm like:
'Oh yeah?'

(*Beat.*)

But does he – ?
Fuck.
'How would you like to meet the people you did this to?'
Just like that.
Right between the eyes.

(*Beat.*)

'I'm sorry?
Do what?'

(*Beat.*)

'Meet the victims,' he says.
'The parents of the child.'
And he sits there with this smile on his face
Like he's just offered me tickets to the football.
'So what's in it for me?'
I say.
'What's in it for me?'

(*Beat.*)

And there's this
Crafty look on his face:
'Are you ready to face your future?'

(*Beat.*)

'Yeah,' I say.
'I think I am.'

(*Beat.*)

'But I'm hearing good things about you,
Leon.'
'Such as what?'
'Such as all these pictures you're painting.
Is there nothing else you'd like to share with these good
people?
Nothing else you'd like to tell them,
Now you've had the chance to think about
What it is you've done?'

(*Beat.*)

'Look mate,
Let's cut the crap.
I done four years.
So I'll ask you a question, shall I?
How would you like to be run over by your own car?'

(*Beat.*)

That knocks the smile off his face.
He doesn't look very happy now, does he.

(*Beat.*)

'Look, boss,
I just want to get out.
I just want to get out, all right?'

(*Beat.*)

'Well,' he says,
'There's getting out,
And getting out.
What exactly are you going to be doing,
When you get out?'

Scene Fourteen

Petra *alone, after* **Casey***'s departure.*

Petra
So when he's left,
When we've said our piece,
I see what I always see:
Another person,
A do-gooder,
A visitor to the shrine.
But it's not their shrine, is it:
So what can they say
When they know
No holy words?

Scene Fifteen

Leon *in jail: a speech delivered as much to his own interiority, as for the benefit of* **Casey***.*

Leon
(*grandly*)
'When I Get Out',
By Leon.

(*Beat.*)

OK,
I've thought about it.
I've thought a lot about it,
Mr Casey.

(*Beat.*)

I'm not afraid of work,
I'm not afraid of getting my hands dirty.
You get an apprenticeship in a garage.
They pay you while you get your level one.
Stick your hands down the bonnet of a car.
Like being a vet,
Except this one's got wheels,
Farts black smoke!
Grease up to your elbow:
On your cock
When you go for a slash.
I'd get one of those souped-up racing engines,
Stick it on to a Fiesta.
You know, something
Turbo-charged,
Fuel-injected,
Which means the air gets right in there,
Where the petrol burns.
Not difficult if you know how,
If you've got your basic welding.

(*Beat; now positioning himself.*)

Tail fins sloping round behind,
Twin exhausts coming out the back.
Dashboard like a bloody,
Bloody –
Jet plane!
Are you watching, Mr Casey?
Then watch this!
Cos this is me taking off.
This is me flying!
Right out of here.
Right out of this fucking place.

(*Pause.*)

Goes on my record, right?

If I agree to meet them:
It goes on my record, yeah?

Scene Sixteen

We are back at the conference. But late on now. The first, expository
stages are over.

Petra
(emphatic, stating her purpose)
Now that it's my turn to speak
I think I should warn everybody:
I'm not here to be nice.
And I find it striking
How, in all this careful arrangement of people and chairs,
My daughter is the only one who hasn't been invited.
So is that OK with everyone?
If I invite her?

(She brings a chair and places it.)

There.
This will be her chair.
Charley's chair.
She's going to be ten next week.
We remember her birthday.
Don't we, Jimmy?

Scene Seventeen

Cut to a subsequent preparative meeting between **Leon** *and* **Casey**,
a fortnight, perhaps, after the first. **Leon** *in jail.*

Leon
If I agree to meet them,
If I do, Mr Casey:
There's just one thing I want to ask.
Freddie died cos he wasn't wearing a safety belt,
And that was his look-out.
But from what I heard,
Their kid died because she was in the front seat.

And that was an offence what they did.
My lawyer told me
They were lucky not to be charged.
So what I want to ask is:
Why was she there
Where she should never have been?
I need to know that, Mr Casey.
I have a right to know.

(*Beat.*)

So that's it.
If I agree to meet them,
If I do:
It's because I'm thinking about my future, too.
Which is what you want, isn't it?

Scene Eighteen

Back to the conference.

Petra
(*abruptly, to* **Leon**)
So tell me:
When you do get out,
Are you intending to visit us again?

Leon
Don't know what you mean.

Petra
I mean,
Are you coming back?
Is there anything else you want from us?

Leon
No.

Petra
Are you sure?

Leon
Yes.

Petra
What makes you so sure?
Cars?
Money?
Possessions?

Leon
I'm not doing it again.

(*Small pause.*)

Petra
This car you stole:
The car that killed our daughter.
Did you know,
That the development you broke into,
The estate you described to us in your account,
It happened to be our home.
It was where we lived.
Did you know that?

Leon
No.

Petra
Well, who can blame you for that?
It's just one of those things.

Leon
I didn't know.

Petra
Well, how could you have known?
In the heat of the moment?

Leon
Yeah, I didn't know.

                    Petra
              So this place:
              Our home.
          Would it surprise you
          That we moved there
          To bring up our family?

Jimmy
(*seeing the way she's going*)
Petra.

                    Petra
          Well, that's why people move
              To places like that,
          Why should we be any different?
      A family estate without graffiti on the walls
          Or gob on the pavements.
          A place where children can play.
              He must have seen that.
              He'd cased the joint.
              You'd cased the joint,
                  Hadn't you?
          You'd seen the cars through the gate.

Leon
Yeah.
Yeah, we'd seen the cars.

                    Petra
          So what could be more natural?
              I mean,
      I think I completely understand what you're driving at,
          If you'll pardon the pun.
          You saw where we lived,
              What we had,

And you thought:
'That's easy pickings.
That's fair game.'

Leon
No.
We just come for the car.

Petra
You just *come* for the car?

Leon
Yeah,
That's what I'm saying.

Petra
But you never
Just come for the car.
Isn't it obvious?
You come to break into somebody else's home,
You come to break into somebody else's life!

Leon
And I'm sorry!

Petra
You're sorry?

(*Beat; then savage.*)

You know, Jimmy,
I think I'd have respected him more
If he'd broken in and taken her
Like any regular child-snatcher.

Leon
But I didn't take her!
I didn't take anybody./

Jimmy
All right, Petra.

Leon
I didn't come to take anyone.
It's what I'm telling you.
I just wanted a car.
A nice car.

> **Petra**
> A nice car?
> You mean
> A car with tits?

Leon
What?

> **Petra**
> A car you could fuck.

Leon
What are you talking about?
What is she talking about?

> **Petra**
> You see,
> This is the point.
> It's just another story, isn't it,
> Another picture he's preparing
> For the judge:
> *He just wanted a nice car.*
> So he comes to where the nice cars are.
> Where else?
> What could be more natural than that?
> I mean,
> There we were,
> Daring to live in a place
> Like that.

Leon
What's she saying?/

     Petra
     I'm saying:

Leon
I don't understand what she's saying.

     Petra
     I haven't come here to be nice.
     And I'm not allowing this lie
     To go unchallenged.
     This lie,
     This picture you're painting:
     That somehow,
     You had no choice.
     That what you did was understandable.
     That people like us
     Deserve to be preyed upon
     By people like you.

Leon
What's people like me?/

     Petra
     We all have choices.

Leon
What's people like me?

     Petra
     Little arseholes
     Who choose to take a car,
     As though it had no more consequence than
     Lifting a shopping trolley from Sainsbury's.
     You choose to take a car –
     A car you can't properly handle

And drive it at high speed
Along a road you don't know.
And then you take a life.
Two lives!
And this is a direct result,
If anyone cares to look –
There's this simple,
Straight line from one act
To the next.
You didn't just
Take a car.
You killed my child!
And I'm not letting you off the hook.
I'm not letting you walk away
As though it were just some accident.
You're not just walking away from this!

Leon, *angered now, rises to fetch a second chair, which he places in opposition to* **Charley***'s, so the two empty chairs face each other.*

Jimmy
What's he doing?

Leon
What about Freddie?
Does he get a chair and all?

Petra
Is this supposed to be a joke?

Jimmy
What's he doing, Mr Casey?

Leon
Same as what they're doing.
I'm doing what they're doing.
Freddie can sit by me, Mr Casey.
Maybe he has something to say, too.
He's dead too, remember?

Jimmy
It's not the same, Leon./

Leon
So what's not the same?
He's dead too.

Jimmy
Freddie was an accomplice.
A victim of his own behaviour.
Our daughter was innocent.

Leon
So why not tell him that.
Tell him
What you keep telling me.
Ask *him* why he came knocking on my window that night.
Ask *him* why he was in the passenger seat,
And not me.
Ask *him* for a change!

Jimmy
No,
I don't think you understand.

Petra
(*over* **Jimmy**, *to* **Casey**)
So tell him, Mr Casey,
Because unless he can understand that
We might as well pick up our things and go.

Leon
(*to* **Casey**)
But I'm not trying to say
What they think I'm saying.

Jimmy
So what are you saying?

Leon
It was an accident!

Petra
(*indicating the empty chair*)
So tell her that!
Go on:
Stand up and tell her that!

Jimmy
You've stolen more cars
Than we've had hot dinners, Leon.
You were going to kill someone sooner or later.
Did you never stop to think about that?

Leon
Yeah.
I thought about it.

Jimmy
You thought about it?
Well, you must have thought a lot about it, Leon,
Because it wasn't just that night was it,
And it wasn't just that car.
It could have been any night,
And any bloody car.
And you could have killed anybody.

(*Beat.*)

But you knew that, didn't you?
Because you'd *thought* about it.

Leon
(*beat*)
What can I say?
What do you want me to say?
That it was a rush?
It was a buzz?
It gave me a hard-on?

Jimmy
Jesus Christ!

Leon
You know what?
If I could,
I'd change everything.
I'd put me there, instead of her.
I'd put me there instead of Freddie.
I'd kill me now and bring them two back to life.
That's the truth.
But you don't want to hear that, do you.
You want to hear that I'm some kind of monster,
Some kind of perv.
And I don't blame you.
How could I?
So what can I say that would make any difference?

Jimmy
You can show us what this actually means to you.

Leon
But I just have.

Jimmy
Then you'll have to show us again, won't you.
Because we just don't believe you.

Leon
The pictures, Mr Casey!
Tell them about the pictures!

Jimmy
The pictures?
The pictures?
Where are the scars, Leon?
Show me what hell looks like!

(*Beat.*)

Oh! You can't do that, can you.
Because no one can teach you to draw that.

Petra
You know,
I think it's perfectly clear
What's going on here:
The pictures!
I think we understand each other perfectly.

Leon
So what do you want me to do?
Tell me what it is,
And I'll try to do it.
I swear I'll try.

Petra
Then try this, Leon.
Try this!
Just in case you think for one moment
That we should be grateful
For your being here –
For this *picture* of your remorse –
Listen to this.

(*Beat.*)

You think there's a bottom to it, don't you.
You think that we've reached that now,
Seeing as you're here,
Telling us how apologetic you are.
How very *sorry*.
As if everything comes to rest on something,
Eventually –
Like you falling out of that chair,
Or me chucking a stone down a well –
When you hear the splash back,

Or you hit the floor.
Do you know what I'm talking about?

(*Beat.*)

But it's not.
It's not like that.

(*Beat.*)

When you lose a child,
There is no floor.
There's no sound to tell you
She's arrived.
There's no depth
At which she comes to rest,
At which we can finally say:
'She's OK now.
She's with God now.'

(*Beat.*)

Because how can she be,
When she's in the space between us now.
When she's between me and Jimmy,
And me and you –
And me and me and me.

(*Beat.*)

She's with me all the time,
Telling me
Her death was unnecessary for all sorts of reasons.
So how can she be at rest?
How can she possibly be at rest?

(*Beat.*)

And you haven't told us anything:
Nothing that we didn't know.

(*to* **Casey**)

He's given us nothing,

Mr Casey.
Nothing!

Leon
(*beat; then softly, to the whole room*)
So why was she in the front seat?

Petra
(*rising to go*)
Look, I really think we've heard enough.

Leon
I have a right to know./

Petra
No, you don't,
You really don't.

Leon
But why?
Why?

Petra
We have nothing further to discuss with him, Mr Casey.
It's over.
This whole conversation is finished.

Leon
Then maybe I should be talking to *her*./

Jimmy
No.

Leon
Maybe I should be asking her.

Jimmy
He's not going near that chair.

Petra
Jimmy, it's over.

Jimmy
You're not going near that chair.
You understand?
I said,
Do you understand?

Leon
I just want to know.
I have the right to know.

Petra
You have a right to nothing.
You have no rights over us.

(*Summoning him.*)

Jimmy.
Jimmy!

(*Small pause.*)

Jimmy
It was me.
It was me who let her ride in the front seat.

Petra
Jimmy?

Jimmy
No,
I put my hand up to that.

Petra
But you don't have to put your hand up
To anything!

Jimmy
No, I do.
Cos that's what's killing me.
That's what's poisoning me./

Petra
How can you say that?

Jimmy
Listen to me, Petra!

Petra
No:
This is not what we came to discuss.
You promised me:
We weren't coming here to forgive.

Jimmy
I'm not forgiving him anything.
But there's not one day passes,
Not one single day when I don't hate myself for it.

Petra
You were tired. You wanted to get home!

Jimmy
Oh, we were always tired,
Because we were always working.
We worked so bloody hard
That our own daughter saw more of the child-minder
Than she got to see of her own parents.

Petra
Not in front of him!/

Jimmy
I'm not talking to him!
I'm talking to us!
I'm talking to me!

Petra
Not in front of him.

(*Then, beseeching.*)

Jimmy! Jimmy!

Jimmy
I should have been the one to stand up to her that night.
It should have been me!

Leon
(*beat. Then, steely, to* **Jimmy**)
I'm sorry.
I'm really sorry, mister.
But when you put your kid in the front seat,
You screwed me too.

Petra
What?
What did you say?

Leon
Why isn't Freddie's family here?
Why isn't my mum here?

Petra
No, hold on a second, what is he saying?

Leon
She's scared, that's why.
Cos Freddie's brothers, they're putting shit into her
letterbox.
Spreading lies round my estate,
Saying it was all my fault what happened./

Petra
Well, whose fault was it?
Would someone mind telling me,
Whose fault it was if it wasn't his!

Leon
Making people think
I get off on killing small kids,
Like I'm some kind of *paedo*.
Do you know what that means?
Do you know what that means in here?
No.
You have no idea.
Why should you?

Petra
You killed my daughter.

Leon
But that's not the whole story, is it.

Petra
What's not the whole story?
That you were driving the car?
That you murdered our child!

Leon
You know what I'm talking about!
You know I didn't mean to hurt no one.
It's what I came here to say.

Petra
That's what you came to say?
That's *all* you came here to say?

Leon
No.
I came here to say sorry.
I came here to listen.
But can you listen?
Can *you* listen to me?

Petra
Jimmy,
We've heard enough.

Leon
(*now by-passing* **Petra**)
Mister, don't you think she'd want to hear it, your daughter?/

Petra
Jimmy!

Leon
That it's not like they're saying.
That it wasn't like that.
Maybe that's something you could do for her right now:
Something you could say to her, to make her feel –
I dunno –
Like she's come to rest.

Petra
Oh, God!

Leon
You could tell her I'm not a child-killer.
I'd really like her to hear that.
Just so she'll know
There were no malice in it,
That I meant her no harm.
Then I swear,
I'll do whatever you like,
Say whatever you like.
I'll go, and I won't come back.
Just so you tell her.
Just so you tell her, mister.
Please.

Petra
(*beat; sensing his weakness*)
Jimmy,
No.

Jimmy
She was my child,
Petra./

Petra
Jimmy,
You have no right!

Jimmy
She was my loss.
My loss
As much as yours!

Petra
But of course she was.

Jimmy
So say it to me.
Give me the words you won't give him.

Petra
What words?
What words?

Jimmy
You know what I'm talking about.
You know!

Petra
(*fending off the truth of this*)
Jimmy,
Whatever you think you've done,
It's for her to forgive you,
Not him.

Jimmy
(*beat: then turning at last to* **Leon**)
All right, Leon,
Then I'll say it for her.
Leon – /

Petra
Jimmy, no!
Anger's all we've got.

Don't you see?
It's all he's left us with.
Whatever you say to him,
You say it for yourself.
Not for me.
Not for Charley.

Jimmy
(*solemn, unstoppable now*)
I can't find it in my heart to forgive you,
And I probably never will.
And what is more,
I hope you've suffered.
God!
I hope you've suffered for what you've done.
But I can just about accept
If I try really bloody hard,
I can just about accept
That what you did,
You didn't mean.

Leon
Thank you, mister!
Oh thank you!

Jimmy
No, don't thank me.
Don't thank me!
The only reason
I don't knock you out, boy,
Is that I can't hate you
As much as I hate myself.
You understand that?
Can you understand that?

Leon
Yes.
Yes, I can.

Jimmy
I'm so angry.
I'm so angry I scare myself.
I'm so *angry*!

Petra
Then show *me*, Jimmy.
Show *me*!

Jimmy
(*turning at last to her*)
God's my witness, Petra!
I've been up the drive.
I've stood outside the gate,
On frosty mornings,
When I called in sick at work.
I drove all the way out to see him,
So I'd know where I'd stand
When they let him out:
When his mum pulls up in her car,
Or a taxi comes to take him away.
I'd be there with a gun in my hand.
I swear to God!

(*Small pause. Then to* **Leon**.)

You've taken our daughter, Leon.
And ever since that day
Petra and me,
We've been living this life,
This apology for a life.
So I'm thinking:
You're not taking her along with it.
You're not taking my marriage
Without paying
A terrible fucking price.

(*Beat.*)

But you know what I think?

I think you're irrelevant, now.
I think,
You're just what happened.
You're just –
An accident.
And maybe you should never have been born
But you were –
You were born.
So what would be the use in killing you
When you can't kill an accident?

(*Small pause.*)

And Petra
You don't hate him like you think you do.
Cos it's me you hate.

Petra
That's nonsense, Jimmy.

Jimmy
No it's not!
It's not./

Petra
Don't, Jimmy,
Please.

Jimmy
You hate me for it.
And I'm a dead man.
We're both dead,
Till you give me the words
I'm trying to give him.

Petra
What words?
What words can we possibly give him?

Jimmy
Let him go, Petra.
We have to let him go.

Petra
Jimmy!
No, Jimmy,
Listen!
Whatever it is
You think you've done:
Don't you think she'd forgive you for it?

Leon
But that's not what he's saying!/

Petra
(*to* **Leon**, *trying to shut him out*)
Go away.
Shut up.
You're no part of this.

Leon
Listen to him!
That's not what he's saying!
He's saying:

(*Beat. Insistent now, as though speaking for* **Jimmy**, *but also, most deeply, for himself.*)

'I can't go.
Where can I go?'
He's saying he can't go nowhere
Until you let him!
He's saying:
'This thing I've done,
I can't do nothing.
I can't say nothing.
Cos what can I say?
What can I do?'
He's saying:

(*Beat.*)

He can't.

(*Beat; truly struggling for himself now.*)

He's saying:

(*Beat.*)

I can't!

Leon *stands directly before her now, speechless with the impossibility of what he's asking.* **Petra** *slaps him hard across the face. The relief of the physical gesture for them both is sudden and immense. He takes it without flinching, falling to his knees before her.*

Petra
(*to* **Leon**)
What are you doing?
What's he doing, Jimmy?
Mr Casey?

Leon *clings to her. She raises her arms awkwardly, as if refusing to touch him.*

Petra
Oh, God!
Jimmy,
What's he doing?

Then suddenly, there is nowhere for her to go, but towards **Leon**. *And the moment she touches his head, he comes to her at once, crumbling into her as a child, sobbing with the relief of it. And as a mother she embraces him, as though taking in to herself not just* **Leon**, *but* **Jimmy** *himself.*

Petra
(*to* **Leon**)
You fucking fucker.
You stupid fucking fucker.

(Pause.)

Now go.
Leave us.
Please go,
And don't ever come back.

Leon *rises. He moves deferentially to one side, leaving* **Petra** *and* **Jimmy** *together. Their relationship has changed, as if the moment of her transformation is also the moment of her deepest turning away from him. And they both see this. So they can't come together. Instead, they stand at opposite ends of the space.*

Petra
Oh Jimmy!
Jimmy,
I'm so sorry.

Scene Nineteen

The following scene depicts two divided narratives: the therapeutic dialogue between **Petra** *and* **Jimmy** *intercut by the remainder of* **Leon**'s *expository narrative from earlier in the conference.*

Petra
(softly)
My first reaction,
My first mother's need –

(Beat; then, as if reawakening to the thought of it.)

Yes!
I remember now.
I didn't care what she looked like.
I didn't care about the damage.
I just had to see her.

Leon

So Freddie gets the rod out.
Starts poking it through the letter box,
Right in
Till it's up to the handle.
And suddenly there's a Land Rover parking up.
And a bloke gets out.
But Freddie's still on the end of that rod
With his tongue hanging out.
And I can see this bloke,
This fat bloke
Walking towards us.

Jimmy

(*reluctant to do this, halting*)
At the hospital:
When I realised what had happened.
When I realised
That she'd gone.
Well,
I tried to get up.
I tried to get out of my bed
But the doctors wouldn't let me./

Leon

Fat bloke's seen us,
He starts shouting
'Hey you two!' he says.
But Freddie's got the end of the rod in his hands
And at the very tip
There's this bunch of keys./

Jimmy

Instead they put a needle into me
So I wouldn't get up.
Because I had a fractured pelvis,
And my chest injuries, well –

Leon
So we're away, aren't we,
Ducking and diving
With the keys,
These keys jangling in Freddie's hands,
Till we get to the car
And I'm feeling,
This is living,
You know?
This is really living!

Jimmy
But I swear I would have crawled on my knees
If they'd let me, Petra.
If only they'd let me.

Petra
Jimmy!

Jimmy
So I say,
'At least bring me the body.
At least show me the body!'

Leon
And before we get in,
Before we get to the car,
Freddie chucks me the keys:
'*You drive,*' he says.
'*You!*'
He don't give me no reason,
He just chucks me the keys.
So I do.
So it's me who's driving,
Not him.
So it's him in the passenger seat,
Not me!

Petra
When the police bring me there:
When I get to the hospital –
It would have been
Ten o'clock.
They let me hold her in my arms.
They'd bandaged her up,
So I couldn't see the marks.
They'd put so many bandages on her –
Across her little body –

Jimmy
But they wouldn't let me.
Why was that?
Instead,
They put me under,
You see?
But I'm fighting
As I go,
I'm shouting
As I go:
'At least show me the body!
At least show me the body!'

Leon
So I drive./

Jimmy
No.
No!

Leon
See the fat bloke in the rear view – /

Jimmy
I'm seeing it again.

Petra
Jimmy,
Stop.

Jimmy
But I can't stop.
I can't stop!

Leon
He's got a phone out.
And he's shouting
He's wetting himself.
And there's this shut gate in front of us
So what are we going to do now?
But for some reason it opens,
I mean, the gate opens for us!
It's like Ali Baba!
Well, we're away, aren't we,
Down the road,
We're flying,
We're on a jet plane –
Freddie beside me:
'Go on mate!' he says,
'Let's see what you can do!
Go on!'
Cos this is our chance:
One fat fucking chance
To take something back!

(*Beat.*)

Then all of a sudden
I'm overtaking
Blind corner
Knew you shouldn't
But the adrenalin
It's just pumping me up.
I'm so excited,
I'm so excited
I can't explain.
And then we hear the siren./

Jimmy
God.

Leon
Freddie says:
'The pigs!'/

Jimmy
Oh Christ.

Leon
'We got to lose the pigs!'/

Jimmy
I know what's about to happen,
I know exactly what's about to happen.

Leon
And he's laughing,
And I'm laughing
Cos we know
We can do it.
We just got to get to the strip.
If we can get there
We'd be all right.
We'll torch it.
So what's going to stop us now?
It's our lucky day,
It's our lucky night, isn't it!
So I start accelerating,
Move down into third,
Like you do.
And I'm surging past this Toyota
When out of nowhere – /

(*Simultaneously.*)

Jimmy	**Leon**
Here we go:	Lights in my eyes.
This car on the wrong side	Freddie shouting
of the road;	Brakes screaming,
What the hell?	Car coming in the opposite
I mean,	direction
What the hell is a car doing	And I can't swerve
there?	Cos I'm all boxed in
So I'm slamming on the	By a car on my left –
brakes	The only thing,
But I can't see properly –	The only thing I can do
I can't see anything.	Is to slam the brakes down –
Then there's this noise –	But I can't brake, can I,
This terrible noise.	Cos we're going into a skid.

(*Pause.*)

Jimmy
(*as someone falling from a cliff edge*)
Slow motion.
It's how you remember it.
When everything,
The whole world
Starts plunging,
Plunging.
And I'm plunging too,
I'm falling too.
Till there's nothing between me
And what's coming up.
Till
Almost:
Almost the moment,
The moment before I hit the ground –
That moment:
That's the moment
When I stop –
When I stop falling.

(*Beat.*)

But where am I?
I don't know where I am.
I'm just –

(*Beat.*)

I'm just hanging.

(*Small pause.*)

Petra
Jimmy.
She slipped like a little doll through the safety belt,
And there was nothing you could do.
Nothing!

(*Beat.*)

And her body when I saw it –
It was like the day she was born to us, Jimmy,
She was
A little baby again,
All bound up with cloths!

Jimmy
(*consciousness reviving*)
But when I come to,
I'm not noticing my pain,
I'm hearing this incredible noise,
This blaring noise.
And when I look round to see:

Petra
So I put her on my breast
And I remember now –
I remember feeling
Among the grief –
Among this incredible pain,
This love, Jimmy!

Jimmy
(*vivid with fear*)
Charley!
Charley!
Oh for the love,
For the love of God!

Leon
And then I come round.
Maybe two.
Maybe five.

Jimmy
I'm in the seat again.
And everything's moving up,
Moving up so fast,
I'm shouting – /

Leon
I don't know
I don't know
Where I am./

Jimmy
'Stop!
Why doesn't anyone stop!'

Leon
So I try to get out.
But I can't.

Jimmy
And I'm shouting but there's nobody there.
Except this other voice,
This *boy's* voice
Shouting back:

Leon
(*screaming, terrified, emasculated by fear*)
Freddie!
Freddie!

Jimmy
And that's when I look over my shoulder
And see this
Hole in the windscreen –
Christ!
This red hole
Where Charley was sitting.
Oh God!
Oh my Christ God!

Pause. He's done it. He's broken entirely; but he's reached the place. There's nowhere to go now, but towards where she is. And **Petra** *takes him to her now.*

Petra
It's the love that hurts, Jimmy.
It's only the love that hurts now.
So let it come back to you.
Oh, let it come back!

Long pause, signifying the end of something that has been far too long in the coming: something like a real death, at last.

Scene Twenty

Epilogue.

Leon *stands in the presence of* **Mr E**.

Leon
Think I'll do a picture.
Think I'm ready, Mr E.

(Beat.)

I've got this piece of rubbish.
This steaming pile of crap.
I want to get it down while it's still hot.

Petra, *as before* **Charley**'s *shrine now. Beyond her rooted sadness, there is a new note, a new compassion for herself which allows her the necessary distance. This speech, too, is a kind of leave-taking. She is to all intents and purposes alone.*

Petra
She's five when we move house.
You remember things at that age.
You lay down memories like a new wine.

Leon
I've got these words,
These last words to say to Freddie
While I still remember them.

Leon *too gets out a chair. Places it with great deliberation. This is* **Freddie**. *Now, angrily, and without any irony at all:*

Leon
You stupid fucker.
You stupid fucking fucker.

(Beat. Then, anger giving way to remembered fondness.)

Go, Freddie –
Please go.
Go and don't ever come back.

Pause. First **Petra** *moves off, taking her chair. Then* **Leon** *packs up his chair, with a nod to* **Jimmy**, *who sits alone on his.*

Jimmy's *leave-taking is different. He's scared, mainly of the loneliness he senses; but at the same time, anxious to make the journey.*

Jimmy
There's been this late frost.
This patina of frost all over the back garden.
And I'm thinking:
I'm not going into work on a morning like this.
I know this hill where there's bluebells.
I'm going to take my shoes and socks off.
I'm going to get my toes wet.

(*Small pause.*)

Petra?

(*Beat.*)

Petra?

But she doesn't come, and he stands alone, and brave, as the lights come down.

Methuen Drama Student Editions

Jean Anouilh *Antigone* • John Arden *Serjeant Musgrave's Dance*
Alan Ayckbourn *Confusions* • Aphra Behn *The Rover* • Edward Bond
Lear • *Saved* • Bertolt Brecht *The Caucasian Chalk Circle* • *Fear and
Misery in the Third Reich* • *The Good Person of Szechwan* • *Life of Galileo* •
Mother Courage and her Children• *The Resistible Rise of Arturo Ui* • *The
Threepenny Opera* • Anton Chekhov *The Cherry Orchard* • *The Seagull* •
Three Sisters • *Uncle Vanya* • Caryl Churchill *Serious Money* • *Top Girls*
• Shelagh Delaney *A Taste of Honey* • Euripides *Elektra* • *Medea*•
Dario Fo *Accidental Death of an Anarchist* • Michael Frayn *Copenhagen*
•John Galsworthy *Strife* • Nikolai Gogol *The Government Inspector* •
Robert Holman *Across Oka* • Henrik Ibsen *A Doll's House* • *Ghosts*•
Hedda Gabler • Charlotte Keatley *My Mother Said I Never Should* •
Bernard Kops *Dreams of Anne Frank* • Federico García Lorca *Blood
Wedding* • *Doña Rosita the Spinster* (bilingual edition) •*The House of
Bernarda Alba* • (bilingual edition) • *Yerma* (bilingual edition) • David
Mamet *Glengarry Glen Ross* • *Oleanna* • Patrick Marber *Closer* • John
Marston *Malcontent* • Martin McDonagh *The Lieutenant of Inishmore* •
Joe Orton *Loot* • Luigi Pirandello *Six Characters in Search of an Author*
• Mark Ravenhill *Shopping and F***ing* • Willy Russell *Blood Brothers*
• *Educating Rita* • Sophocles *Antigone* • *Oedipus the King* • Wole
Soyinka *Death and the King's Horseman* • Shelagh Stephenson *The
Memory of Water* • August Strindberg *Miss Julie* •J. M. Synge *The
Playboy of the Western World* • Theatre Workshop *Oh What a Lovely
War* Timberlake Wertenbaker *Our Country's Good* • Arnold Wesker
The Merchant • Oscar Wilde *The Importance of Being Earnest* •
Tennessee Williams *A Streetcar Named Desire* • *The Glass Menagerie*

Methuen Drama Modern Plays

include work by

Edward Albee
Jean Anouilh
John Arden
Margaretta D'Arcy
Peter Barnes
Sebastian Barry
Brendan Behan
Dermot Bolger
Edward Bond
Bertolt Brecht
Howard Brenton
Anthony Burgess
Simon Burke
Jim Cartwright
Caryl Churchill
Complicite
Noël Coward
Lucinda Coxon
Sarah Daniels
Nick Darke
Nick Dear
Shelagh Delaney
David Edgar
David Eldridge
Dario Fo
Michael Frayn
John Godber
Paul Godfrey
David Greig
John Guare
Peter Handke
David Harrower
Jonathan Harvey
Iain Heggie
Declan Hughes
Terry Johnson
Sarah Kane
Charlotte Keatley
Barrie Keeffe

Howard Korder
Robert Lepage
Doug Lucie
Martin McDonagh
John McGrath
Terrence McNally
David Mamet
Patrick Marber
Arthur Miller
Mtwa, Ngema & Simon
Tom Murphy
Phyllis Nagy
Peter Nichols
Sean O'Brien
Joseph O'Connor
Joe Orton
Louise Page
Joe Penhall
Luigi Pirandello
Stephen Poliakoff
Franca Rame
Mark Ravenhill
Philip Ridley
Reginald Rose
Willy Russell
Jean-Paul Sartre
Sam Shepard
Wole Soyinka
Simon Stephens
Shelagh Stephenson
Peter Straughan
C. P. Taylor
Theatre Workshop
Sue Townsend
Judy Upton
Timberlake Wertenbaker
Roy Williams
Snoo Wilson
Victoria Wood

Methuen Drama Contemporary Dramatists

include

Methuen Drama World Classics

include

Jean Anouilh (two volumes)
Brendan Behan
Aphra Behn
Bertolt Brecht (eight volumes)
Büchner
Bulgakov
Calderón
Čapek
Anton Chekhov
Noël Coward (eight volumes)
Feydeau (two volumes)
Eduardo De Filippo
Max Frisch
John Galsworthy
Gogol
Gorky (two volumes)
Harley Granville Barker
  (two volumes)
Victor Hugo
Henrik Ibsen (six volumes)
Jarry

Lorca (three volumes)
Marivaux
Mustapha Matura
David Mercer (two volumes)
Arthur Miller (six volumes)
Molière
Musset
Peter Nichols (two volumes)
Joe Orton
A. W. Pinero
Luigi Pirandello
Terence Rattigan
  (two volumes)
W. Somerset Maugham
  (two volumes)
August Strindberg
  (three volumes)
J. M. Synge
Ramón del Valle-Inclán
Frank Wedekind
Oscar Wilde

For a complete catalogue
of Methuen Drama titles
write to:

Methuen Drama
Bloomsbury Publishing Plc
36 Soho Square
London W1D 3QY

or you can visit our website at:

www.methuendrama.com

Printed in the USA
CPSIA information can be obtained
at www.ICGtesting.com
LVHW020848171024
794056LV00002B/451